Balancing Fa Financial F

HOW TO CREATE A LIFESTYLE AND FINANCIAL FREEDOM WITHOUT SACRIFICING FAMILY TIME

VINCENT HOVORKA

To everyone who wants more from life. Especially for people who wants to spend more time with their families and loved ones. I decided to be and spend as much time as I want to be with my amazing daughters and lovely wife and I wish you will find the same strength as I did. I will help you with that.

And to my wife Barbora and my children Stepanka and Eliska, thank you for loving me and being with me. You are the greatest thing in my life. I am on this journey especially because of you.

Thank you

Contents

Introduction

I wrote this book to share my knowledge of what I have learned in the past few years and what helped me to move to the next level in my life. I truly believe this book can help you to achieve your dreams and start looking at the world with a different set of glasses. I spent too much time trying to be successful, rich and spend time with my family, but it has never worked for me until I changed my mindset. I want to share this with you so you can also go to the next level in your life and be happy and fulfilled. This is my first book in which I will focus mainly on how important family is to me and I think to all of us. Also, the book is focused on what is my way to becoming financially free, and if you also want to achieve this freedom you are very welcome to go on this journey with me. I spent a lot of time trying to be successful in my business and I am doing OK, but it is far away from financial freedom. I was studying and learning for many years from people who achieved this level in their lives and I would love to show you what options we have. I have decided to go along the path which I think everybody can. You don't have to build big businesses or have a lot of money to start. The best thing is I will show you the way that everybody – even with no money to start with – can get to this level in life. But I will also show you what I have learned as I saw a lot of people earn a lot of money but they don't spend much time with their families or they are not healthy. I want to show you that you need to find balance in all areas in your life so you will feel fulfilled. I really hope this book will help you to start thinking differently so we can move towards our dreams together.

Goals?

Recommendations VS Reality

(Our goals can only be reached through a vehicle of a plan, in which we must fervently believe, and upon which we must vigorously act. There is no other route to success. —Pablo Picasso)

If you have ever watched any motivational videos or have been on any good seminars you will have heard that goals are important in order to succeed. And I definitely agree, but how to accomplish all these things you want and still be at home with your family? Your kids need you and I think you want to be with them to see them grow.

One of the goals that I set was to go for a run every morning at 6am. So I started and everything went well, but after a few days my youngest daughter woke up and started crying. I quickly went to bring her to our bed but in the meantime my older daughter woke up as well and she wanted me to stay as she didn't want to be alone in her room. So what would you do? She is my daughter, I love her. Of course I stayed with her and I didn't go for my run.

Another day when my youngest daughter woke up and I brought her back to our room I couldn't move as I didn't want to wake her up again.

After few days trying I just stopped going running. And I was thinking I will start again once they grow older, but this is not a good idea as I want to work on myself now. So what shall I do?

I should probably go for my run after work, but again the kids are so excited to see me so I start playing with them and suddenly it is dinner time. I am thinking that after the kids go to the bed I can go for my run but I am usually tired after a long day at work so I don't go.

These things that I am writing are true but let's be honest, these are excuses and excuses.

Do you want to tell me you can't find fifteen minutes a day for yourself? If you don't give yourself a little time every day for growing you will never live a fulfilled life. Growing can be different for each person. If someone is athletic, fit and strong but their marriage is struggling he or she should find the time for his wife or husband. Or if you are successful in business, you are rich, and you have time for your family but you are not in a good shape and without energy, you won't be fulfilled and happy in your life.

The key is to find a balance between all areas in our lives:

Area 1 Health/Energy

Area 2 Family/Relationships

Area 3 Success/Significance

Area 4 Money/Business

Area 5 Growing

Area 6 Giving

AREA 1

Health and Energy

("The human body is the best picture of the human soul." Tony Robbins)

Health and energy is your fuel to the next level. A car without fuel will get you to the village called NOWHERE. Imagine you are going on a trip by car and you are low on fuel, what will you do? You stop the car at the nearest petrol station and will usually fill the tank. Is it right? Who likes to half fill the tank just to lose time stopping again? But if you take just half a tank your thoughts are: Where is the next petrol station on my way? Will I get there? What are the prices? Is it on the highway or do I need to go to the city? You have spent a lot of your valuable time in the car thinking about it. Valuable time? In the car? I am just driving, what else shall I do? You may be asking these questions but the car is perfect for thinking. Especially if you are alone and driving on a longer trip. FOY I call it, FOY. It stands for "Focus On Yourself".

So let's take a full tank at the petrol station so you are certain that you will reach your destination so you stop thinking about it and will free your mind. Now you can decide what you will focus on. We have a full tank and are ready to focus on ourselves. What will we do? You need to decide which area in your life is struggling. And it means you can give 100% to the next chapter to move you to another level. If you would still be thinking about the fuel and next petrol station, how could you focus 100% on your growth, business, family, relationships? You couldn't.

Why are we finding it so easy to understand the car situation but it is so difficult to understand our own life? Our own health? You need to be fit and healthy to have a fulfilled life. Life on your terms. How many times do you find yourself in a situation where you have no energy to do the things you had planned or there are things that your wife wants you to help with? I found myself in this situation hundreds of times. Now we know that a car doesn't go without fuel, so we don't function without fuel called ENERGY. Many people who say they are tired will sit on the sofa and will get energy, but from what? From doing nothing? Energy is emotions. If you have plenty of energy you are feeling good, you have a positive mood, people around you are happy because they are absorbing your energy, they feel with you. How to get this energy then? Emotion comes from motion. You need to move to get energy. If you are feeling empty and without energy I have an answer. MOVE. MOVE RIGHT NOW. I don't care if you are reading this book and you are at home, at school, you are on the train or you are at work behind your desk and should be working but instead reading this. How far did you get at your work with your tasks today? Probably not very far if you are reading instead of working. I think you get me now. And I know you understand you need to move and you need to move RIGHT

NOW. Just stand up and go. Yes, I know. Now you are thinking what will my colleagues think about me or my boss? Stop thinking what they are thinking, you don't play poker in here. You want more energy so stand up and go. Don't worry, when you come back your tank will be full and you can fully focus on your work and you will get further in the next hour than you did in the last few days. And if the boss comes and asks you what just happened, where you have been for the last fifteen minutes? Just tell him the truth. I felt I was not getting good results so I needed energy to function better, so have a look at my results now. If you are in a good work environment no-one will mind you going for a ten-minute run if they see you are doing it to be a better employee, better student or better person.

Did you move at all or are you still sitting in your chair and reading instead of acting? GO, GO now. I am serious because if you want to improve in other areas of your life you need to have energy. Without it you can stop reading right now and bin the book. Make a decision and make it NOW. I am not just saying these things, just now I did push ups and I was jumping as high as I could to get an energy boost. And I am feeling great and ready to move to the next chapter.

AREA 2

Family and Relationships

("Think of your family today and every day thereafter, don't let the busy world of today keep you from showing how much you love and appreciate your family." –Josiah)

If you are still reading this book, congratulations. You have got to the next level and the best thing is you have the energy to focus on it.

Relationships

Let's start with relationships first. Intimate relationships are very important. I will tell you my story so you will understand how difficult they can be, and if you don't master this part of your life you won't be happy and will definitely not be fulfilled.

I was fourteen years old and I met my first love. I have never had a good opinion about myself, especially about my looks. Then I started dating her and I had no clue how it happened as she was beautiful and I was amazed by her. But as time passed I was more and more in love with her and she knew I was. So whatever she wanted me to do I did. And because it starts slowly you don't even realise how bad it can go and how big it can grow. She was cheating on me and I forgave her and stayed, that was how much I loved her. She wanted me to change my classes at school so I could be in the same ones as her, so I did. I was very good at maths and she wasn't. She wanted me to help her with tests so I did, but after a while when teacher saw what we were doing we had to stop. I couldn't help her anymore but I didn't want her to feel bad that I am better at something, so I stopped writing the tests so we could have the same evaluation. I moved to her city which was 50 km away from mine. I lived in her grandmother's flat. She was so jealous all the time. I couldn't have female friends and I didn't really have any friends in the city I lived. Every so often I was going to my house back in my city but she could not come with me all the time, and she even started to become jealous about my mother. I was so desperate. I was coming home and crying because my girlfriend was texting me bad messages and I didn't know what to do. I told my mum that she doesn't want me to chat with her so I was speaking with my mum in private at night and asking her not to tell anyone so my girlfriend wouldn't know. Many times when I was very desperate I was thinking it would be easier to be without her, but I loved her. And she was saying she would kill herself if I left her. But it was blind love. But I stayed with her for nearly five years and we got engaged. In those five years of my life I lost all of my friends. I couldn't meet with anyone I used to. I was just with her. But it is not life. It is prison. You can't give one person everything and definitely not all of you. You need to be proud of who you are and either the person likes you as you are or not. Don't let your partner change you because they don't like you, they like the person who you are pretending to be. I was angry, frustrated, desperate and I was blaming her for everything she had done to me. But the truth is I was stupid to allow it to happen.

This was my bad experience in a relationship. And if you are going through something similar in your life you won't be happy in other areas of your life if you don't figure this one out. Where to start? How to find the right partner for you? Or, if you have one, is she or he the right fit for you?

Start with writing a list of priorities. For example:

My priorities	My partner priorities
Family	Look Good
Help others	Party Life
Business	Friends
Travel	Travel
Be Famous	Smoking
Health	Drinking
	Family

Once you have written your own list and your partner's list of priorities have a proper look.

If two of your main priorities are the same there is a big chance you will succeed in your relationship because you want to go the same way. You want to take the same path towards your brighter future and you can talk about these things and be fully open. If you have at least one priority the same there is still a good chance your relationship will work but it will take a bit of work and patience. If there are none get out of this relationship quickly or don't even start with that person. Approximately 95% success in any relationship is the people who you select. And it is true in every area in your life whether it be work or partner. I will give you an example. I have a food business. I have had a number of employees in the past and at interview a person appears to be good. The first few weeks pass and the person is still doing good. But as time goes the person starts showing up late at work or not doing their job properly. So you are thinking maybe they have some problems in their personal life so you are hoping it will get better in time but the truth is it is getting worse. I was trying to figure out what was happening and I couldn't come to any conclusion. After I did figure it out. I needed to find out what the main priorities of this person are. And I found out that the priorities were very different to mine. Or than what the business needed to be. Her priorities were her partner, another different business where she was in charge, another priority was school, meeting with friends, and somewhere down on the list was my food business. So she didn't give me 100%. And it is my fault as I could have asked her from the beginning what she wants from life, where she is going and what her priorities are, but I didn't. She may be a good person but not a good fit to my business. She is not working for me any longer. I found people who are happy to work for me and they are taking the job seriously and they love what they do.

Family

I have family myself. I have two amazing daughters and a lovely wife. The joy they are bringing me is something so strong that only if you have a family yourself will you understand. I am a very happy husband and father. Compared to the first relationship of my life this one is 100% fulfilled. Of course there are struggles sometimes when the kids are crying, not sleeping, you are not sleeping and things like that. But this is life and this is a part of it. These things which are happening to you can be called problems and that is why you don't feel very good about them. Just change a word and call them challenges. Just yesterday I was putting my one year old daughter to bed and she was crying for at least one and a half hours. I was hugging her, trying to calm her down but nothing worked. And I stayed with her until she fell asleep. When I was lying with her I realised how important it is to use all the time you have to do the right things and focus on what really matters. And that is why I am writing this book because I want to be helping people and have purpose in life, instead of wasting time watching TV or checking social media all the time. What is it bringing to you? Do you feel you are relaxed after that? No, you don't. It may seem that way but what you are really doing is nothing. I watched movies all day long when I didn't have a family and do you know how I felt after a day or two watching? Of course you know because you feel the same. You are more tired than before and in your mind you are saying to yourself, "Why I am even watching that many movies when it is not moving me towards my dreams or goals?" Do you want to have your family and partner happy and fulfilled? Stop doing all these things which are taking you away from them. Start being with them and enjoy every moment which you spend with them. Appreciate every hour and every minute of the time you are with them. Live at this moment. If you are at home, be at home. And I don't mean only your body but I mean your mind. Stop thinking what will happen tomorrow at work or who told you some silly things or what else you need to do tonight. Bin all the garbage from your mind and live NOW. Live with your family at this moment. They will feel you are with them and they will feel better. They will know you are now with them 100%. I know it may sound difficult to stop thinking about all these elements in your life, that is why we need to separate our priorities and focus.

AREA 3

Success and Significance

("Knowing Is Not Enough; We Must Apply. Wishing Is Not Enough; We Must Do." – Johann Wolfgang Von Goethe)

Many people want to be successful. There are plenty of people who succeeded in different roles in their life. Either you want to be a doctor and have your own clinic and feel proud at what you have accomplished, or you want to be lawyer making £10,000 a month, or you want to be the best chess player in your team and become another Kasparov. But the question is are you also wealthy and fulfilled?

Significance and success is important in life as we feel good that we have accomplished what we wanted. But have you got there and still feel empty? That is why you need to master every area in your life. Don't focus only on one or two. Lots of people are focused only on success and money so eventually they will get there, but on the way they forgot who was with them at the start of the journey. There was a partner, family, friends, health. Now you are there on the top of the hill. You are successful and you have plenty of money. But you left your closest behind. You don't feel that way as money attracts people but are these people with you because they like you or your money? For a while you may feel good but let's be honest there is a limit to what you can do. You can be laying all day on the beach but if you are alone or with fake people how do you feel? I am just saying success is a good thing but if you decide to go that way make sure you are taking care about all the other areas in your life. I want to be successful too and I want to feel significant, but I am spreading my time to all the areas in life so I know I didn't leave anything behind. One of the two main things which people leave behind is their health.

AREA 4

Money, Business and Career

("Formal education will make you a living; self-education will make you a fortune. --Jim Rohn")

This is for most people a very important part of their lives. Money is important in our lives and we need to learn to master the game of money. You need to become a chess player, not a pawn. Maybe from the beginning you need to gain experience and confidence so you start as a pawn before going the next step up, or if someone is in the way you cross over him after a while and you become a knight. You are jumping, making bigger moves, feeling more confident what you can do and suddenly you are a bishop. Watching everything from far away, you have better orientation as to what is happening and suddenly you are rook. You are strong and full of energy, you can go far away and you feel safe there as it is hard to attack you. Now you are a queen and you can do and accomplish many things, you can go anywhere you like but you still need to ask your king for permission. As a king you run the show. Without you they couldn't do anything but remember you are just a king. You are on the top and you are trapped. You don't have any strong moves. You are just sitting there and hoping your team will protect you. But if you want them to protect you, you need to be a great leader and encourage them to great things. It is a good feeling to be a king. Once you get on top you feel great. Now is a time for your game. You are becoming a chess player, but you need to be very careful which opponent you will pick because now you are not just in the game, but you are in charge and you make all the decisions which will move you forward, closer to your goals or you will step back and lose everything. Decide if you want to be in someone's game or you want to have your own one. I am not saying one is better than the other one. You just need to find your WHY? Why am I doing the things which I am doing? Is it really what I should do? Am I happy with my situation at work or in my business? Is it bringing me joy and happiness or stress and pain? And if you like some company and you like the idea of what you are doing just work there and you will feel happy because you will be doing what you love. But first you need to figure it out. What do you love? What is your motive for action? Lots of people know what to do but they don't do what they know. Probably you can tell I like chess.

Financial freedom

What is financial freedom or financial independence? Lots of people are working hard, they are working more hours than they should, and they still feel the same. Your salary is rising as you are better in the things you do, but you don't feel a big difference when you have a look at your bank account. You still need to use your credit card every so often as you don't have enough to survive the last few days before payday. Or you are good in saving money and after five years you have saved £10,000 but £10,000 is much less then it was five years ago because of inflation etc… If you really want to master money and be financially free you need to understand a few fundamentals:

1) How is money created?
2) Saving VS investing?
3) Sources of income?
4) Cashflow quadrant
5) Good and bad debt
6) Taxes

How is money created?

To understand this topic we need to have a look back to the past. Exactly to the year 1971 when President Richard Nixon took the dollar to the gold standard. What does it mean exactly? It means until then every dollar was backed up by gold. Since 1971 the dollar doesn't need to be backed up by gold and it means money is no longer money but is called fiat money. Governments are printing money faster than you can imagine. And fiat money will work until people stop believing in it. Then it will lose its power and will be useless like what happened in Germany in 1921 when the government was printing money so fast and hyperinflation occurred, and after they were using this paper just to light up a fire in their fireplaces. I will give you an example so you will understand a little bit better what power gold holds and how fiat money can compete with it. Let's say it is the year 1971 and you have a one ounce gold coin which cost $50 back then. You take the coin and go to the shop and for that you can buy a good-looking suit, nice shoes, suitcase, hat and they will still give you some change in silver coins. If you take the same coin today, which the value is around $1,500, you can buy pretty much the same things. Do you think if you would have saved $50 you could buy these things today? Of course not. So what is happening? Do you think a one ounce gold coin changed over all these years? No, it is not the coin. This is fiat money. They are losing value as the government is printing them as they want. I mean they need to have a reason to print them and it is very easy. Have you been offered a credit card? Are you getting mails every so often from different banks to create one? In shopping centres you can get credit cards, especially for Christmas. They are offering them to everyone so you decide to take one just in case you may use it one day. Now it is the day when you are out of money so you use your credit card and here at this moment you are printing money. I mean the government has reason to print them as people are borrowing. Is it good to save money when we now know it is actually fiat money and is losing its power every minute?

Saving VS investing

Now we know money is not really real any longer and it is just a question of time how long it will last. How long people will trust them, trust governments. Do you still want to save your fiat money when the government is printing it faster than you can even imagine? The fact is that after real estate crashed in 2008 they printed twice that much money. In 2008 the market was on top, there was $700 billion in the system. This money was created a long time ago, slowly when the economy was growing and from 1971 faster as the dollar was taken as gold standard. What number do you think it is now? After twelve years? Yes, I know I told you already twice that much. There is $1.3 trillion in the system right now. Yes, it is fiat money, fake money. Did you also manage to double your savings in the past twelve years? You had $10,000 at the beginning and this $10,000 is now $20,000? No? The reason is we can't save fast enough. Printing is so quick. What other option do we have? We need to learn how to invest our money and there are many ways to do it. You just need to decide what option you would like to take and in which you believe. But before we get to the investing, we need to know from where are you getting your income.

Sources of Income

Earned Income

The most common income is earned income. You have a job and you are paid for the hours you spend in the job, or if you are self-employed you get paid for the work you have done. Most people have just this type of income. This income is OK but there is a one big disadvantage compared to the other sources. There is a line which you can't cross. And this line is called time. You have twenty-four hours in a day. You need to sleep, you have family, etc… So most of the people, if they want to earn more money, will take extra shifts, they work overnight. The more time they spend in the job, the more they earn. But as we said in the beginning, we want to master all areas in our life and we want to be with our family so we need to think what other options we have to make money.

Portfolio Income

Some people are maybe familiar with this type of income. Let's say you will buy a stock from

Microsoft and later on you will sell it and you will make money on it. That is called capital gain and

you have to pay taxes on it. Or you will buy a flat, you will refurbish it and sell it. Again, this is the same situation, this is capital gain and it is taxed. Taxes are the number one expense in our income. In portfolio income you can lower your tax as you can reinvest your gain and it means you don't pay taxes, but you can't just take the money and spend it as you wish.

Passive Income

This type of income is the best as you pay very little on taxes or nothing. The reason why rich people don't pay taxes is because they are not employed, they don't work for earned. They are acquiring assets which are bringing them cashflow.

Cashflow Quadrant

E	B
40%	20%
S	I
60%	0%

E stands for employee. Employee has no control of how much tax he will pay. If you are an employee and you got a raise in the past, have you checked how much more tax are you paying? Or you did more hours than the month before but the money which appeared on your account is similar to the month before. How is this possible? Because the government is taking more every time you work harder, you do extra hours, you don't sleep and you do the night shift, and you are trying very hard but they just tax you more and that is it. So to be an employee has definitely some disadvantages. I am not saying everything is bad. I was an employee in the past. People like to be employees for different reasons so let's have a look what reasons they have so we can talk about them. What is the number one reason? I think people like to feel secure. They have a steady job and they have paid holidays. They feel they have a safety net and nothing can happen to them. But have you ever really checked your contract if you have one? How many months will your safety net hold you? How long is your termination notice? Do you still feel safe at your current job? If not, what changed? Or what will we do about it? And if you have a good position in your company and you are well paid it is even worse if something like that happened as usually people who earn more have bigger expenses. So the question is how long can you survive from your savings? Calculate all your expenses and your savings first. Let say we have £5,000 in savings and our monthly expenses are £2,500. Savings – Expenses = months you are covered for. In our example we would be able to survive two months. Some people don't have any savings so what will they do? It sounds scary but this is the reality. OK, let's have a look to the next box in our quadrant.

S stands for self-employed or it can be a small business. You are for example a doctor and you own you own clinic so you are self-employed. Or you are an electrician and you have a small team of people who are helping you so you have a small business. Why do self-employed people pay the highest taxes? I don't actually know why, but the government wants them to. I have a small business myself and when I started four years ago I thought it was a good thing to do. I could work as I want, I am in charge of my business, and if I am good enough I will have lots of customers and make plenty of money. But I started slowly. A few sales here and there and after two years I started to be more busy and making more money and I thought YES! I am on a good track to success and financial freedom. I realised it is not what I thought. Once my accountant told me how many taxes I have to pay and for what I couldn't believe it. I have to pay: Corporation tax (19%), VAT (20%), Employer contribution (13.8%), Pension Scheme (3%) = 55.8%. When you realise you are actually paying all this to the government it gets ridiculous. Governments want the economy to grow, but I have to say they are not keen to help small businesses or self-employed people. That is why I decided to focus on passive income to pay very little taxes or nothing.

B stands for big business. Big businesses work differently to small ones. The reason is large companies are establishing businesses depending on what governments wants them to do. You can find out online what grants each country is offering and what the government wants to do. They are offering great advantages in areas which they want to improve, so they offer huge tax reliefs and other advantages. So that is why big companies are not paying taxes. They are doing what governments want them to do. They are creating a good relationship with the government as they know they can't beat it. So instead of focusing what the government is doing wrong, try to find out what they are offering which could help you lower your taxes and other aspects in your future business.

I stands for investor. An investor pays 0% on taxes as he knows where to invest and have tax relief. You are thinking how to became an investor right? Anyone can be an investor and you don't have to have millions to become one. You can start with very little and build it up as big as you want. I am exactly here in this spot now. You are not alone. Don't worry. As I mentioned before I have a small business and it is doing OK but the taxes are too much. I decided to change my financial situation and get to the I quadrant. So let's go on this journey together and we can discuss things which will help us to move forward, closer to our goals. You can always visit my Youtube Channel Vincent Hovorka or Instagram page vincent.hovorka and write me a question so I can help you to get to another level on your way to financial freedom. Financial freedom is different for every person. Let's have a look about finances so you can create your own financial freedom. Lots of people want to be financially free but they don't really know what it means or where they should go. We need to have a clear vision before we start acting. Most people have this financial statement.

Income
Job

Expenses
Food
Rent
Fuel
Etc…

Assets	Liabilities
	Credit Cards
	House
	Car
	Etc…

So now you see. The majority of people are living paycheck to paycheck to be able to pay their liabilities. The problem is that bad accountants or bankers tell you that your house or car is an asset. It can be but usually it is not. You need to start thinking. Is the house or car making you money each month or is it doing the opposite? If it is an expense than this is a liability. If you are renting your flat and this is bringing you money back into your pocket this is an asset. Now write your own financial statement so you will know where you are at this moment. Basically where you want to get to is up to you. You will be financially free once your assets will be bringing you enough money to cover all your expenses. And that can be different for all of us. Some people prefer a simple life and don't like to travel or spend much so their monthly expenses are £1,000/month so they need to acquire enough assets to cover it. If you have a family and you love travelling or buying expensive things your number will be different. Every person has a different number. And it doesn't mean you have to stop working if you do what you love. It just mean that you can decide if you are going to work because you want to or because you have to. And this is a very different feeling, especially when you wake up in the morning. I remember when I was younger I hated the feeling that I had to go to school, especially Sunday when you know tomorrow you have to go. Now I have a small business and I love what I do, but I pay too much on taxes and this is the part I don't like. I need to start investing but in the area where it is worthy from a tax perspective. Our financial statement in the future should look like that.

Income	
Expenses	
Food	
Rent	
Fuel	
Etc…	

Assets	Liabilities
Real estates	
Businesses	
Commodities	

How to start when we are working at our current job and have no money for investing? We are happy to survive? Good point, but the best thing in all of that is you don't need money to start. You need to be creative. Start using your muscles and you will figure this out. When I say muscles I mean especially the brain. Ok, I know you are excited to hear about that and how to do it so you can start straightaway, but let's discuss other things before we get to the investing and creating our passive income.

Good and Bad Debt

Did you know that not all debt has to be bad? The problem is that most people think debt is bad. Do you think your credit card is a bad debt? You are probably thinking yes it is because they are charging me 30% APR. And do you think your mortgage is a good debt? These are stupid questions. Of course it is good as I pay just 4% APR which is great, and inflation is around 2% so this a perfect debt. But in the last chapter we were speaking about cashflow and how it affects your financial statement. Is your great mortgage giving you money in your pocket? The same with your credit card. Is it bringing you income or are you paying interest every month? To understand good and bad debt you need to understand that it depends on circumstances. Let's have a couple of examples. I buy a motorbike and I use my credit cards. I am hiring out my motorbike so I get money from it. If the money I receive from hiring out my motorbike is bigger than the money I need to pay back my credit card it means it is a good debt. Do you understand? The percentage is not everything. Of course, if you could buy a motorbike with the same APR as your mortgage even better, but this isn't usually possible. You just need to figure out for what are you using this debt money. Are you acquiring assets or are you just buying more liabilities? I know you are thinking but my accountant told me buy a new car this year so you will lower your taxes and this is a good asset for your household, but is it? I think you can answer this question for yourself now. The reason why most accountants are telling you to buy a new car or buy a bigger house so you will have tax deductible items is that they have no idea there are other options. I am not saying they are giving you bad advice but they just don't know as governments don't want people to know these things. Taxes are the number one income for governments. Most accountants studied in the school system and they got all this information from there, but most of them don't have a business and work as an employee so do not really see things from a self-employed person's perspective. They will tell you it is impossible to pay less and you will probably believe them. But there are ways to legally pay less in tax. Did you know the tax law is only 5% about how to increase your taxes, the remaining 95% is how to deduct them. Believe me. There is a way to do it correctly and you don't have to suffer these tax payments every month as I do. Let's do it the clever way. I think you have an idea about good and bad debt. We will get back to it in examples when we will be investing our (not real) money.

Taxes

I have briefly spoken about taxes already. Taxes are the number one expense in our lives. Imagine one year has 365 days. You are working 330 days. Half of your income you pay in taxes. It means 165 days you are working for yourself and for your family and the other 165 days you are working for the government. Does it sounds fair? How far could you get if all those 330 days would be for your family and yourself? Or you could work your 165 days for your income and the rest of the year you would have holidays. Or you would be doing whatever you like. That is exactly what I am starting to do. I have had enough of hard work and paying so much to the government. Let's learn about taxes and understand them. Do you know how to recognise a good accountant? Ask him a simple question. "How much tax will I pay this year?" A good accountant's answer: "How much would you like to pay?" Usually good accountants are people who are practising what they are advising. They have a business, they have a passive income, they know these things. If your accountant is giving you the same advice every year to buy something to lower your taxes, he is probably not that good. There is not much you can do. You have no control over your taxes, not ever. You can't deduct anything, and each salary increase increases your taxes or tax brackets. Now we need to move from E and S quadrant to B or I quadrant.

B quadrant is pretty hard for a start. As your firm needs to be large and if you are employee or as I am a small business owner, I can't even imagine in the present state how I could have a company with more than 500 employees. Let's skip B quadrant and start focusing on I quadrant.

Investing

Recapitulation of financial statement. We need to know where we are heading.

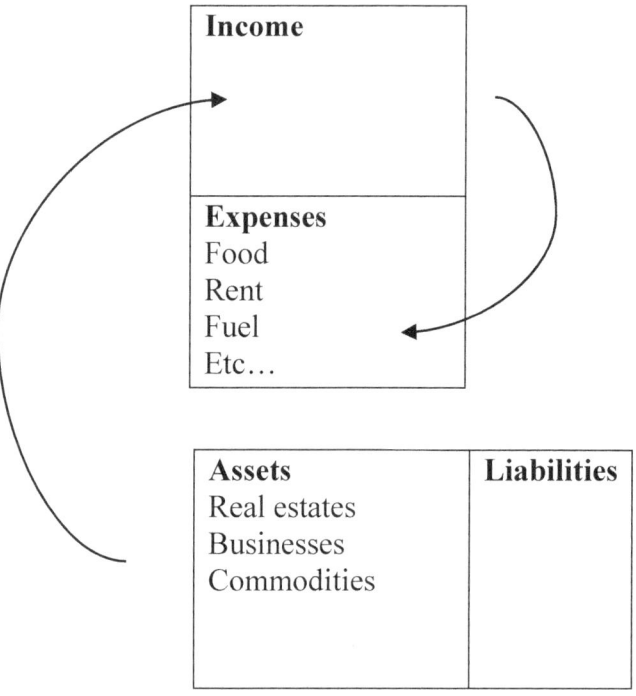

Make a proper financial statement and put in everything you would love to do in your life. If you want to travel once, twice a year, calculate how much this will cost you and divide by twelve so you know how much this will cost you every month. Now we have everything on paper, pin the paper on your board, or put on your fridge, you need to see it. Visualisation is a very strong tool. We will speak more about it later in the book.

Where to invest?

Stock Market, Commodities, Real Estate

Stock Market

Lots of people think if they invest in the stock market they will become rich quickly. They are taking advice from financial consultants, brokers, investing specialists etc… They want you to invest through their mutual fund or use their online tools to invest. There are many things they are not telling you. I will give you a few examples so you have a better idea. They show you brochures where their mutual fund earned 20% profit in the last year, so if you invest £100 at the end of the year you will have £120? Usually this is not true and the reason is they don't tell you how much they are charging to manage your money in the fund. It is usually written in terms and conditions, very small letters and hundreds of pages, so people usually don't give a lot of attention to it. Another thing is they are saying you will get this much money at the end of the year, but most of the people are investing on a monthly basis so if you invest £100 over a twelve-month period you won't have £120 at the end of the year. The biggest expenses are fees to the mutual fund. They are usually hidden. Mutual funds are making money on fees. They may be trying to beat the market, but 96% of mutual funds don't beat the market in a longer period. I will give you an example: An investing specialist comes to your home and makes you an offer. "You invest your money and if we make a profit you will get 40% from it and we keep the rest, and if we don't make any money you will lose but we will still charge you fees anyway." Would you like to sign up? No? There is $17 trillion managed by mutual funds in the USA. You need to study and study hard to understand this topic. Another thing is you need to use your own money to invest which can be risky. If you really want to invest in stocks, learn something before you start.

Commodities

Some people like to invest in commodities and I also like this type of investment. The thing is you need your money to buy something. It can be gold, silver, coffee, etc… As I wrote at the beginning of this book, gold is a great commodity to hold value over time. It is a good long-term investment. Silver is cheaper to buy. Everybody can afford to buy a one ounce silver coin. Check the prices online. Silver is more and more popular in industry, it is used in new cars, robotics, etc… In the future it will be in higher demand and it means silver will increase in value. I personally think it is better to invest in silver than gold. This is only my opinion. Do some research on it and make your own opinion. Remember, real gold and silver is not the same as what you own on paper. If you own it on paper you are dealing in the stock market again. Commodities are a good thing to invest in but we still need our passive income to be financially free, that is why my journey is starting through real estates.

Real Estate

Finally we got to the stage where I am starting investing, and I think if you want to get out of the rat race and be financially free this a good way. It is very difficult to start to talk about this topic as it is quite complex. Let's go step by step so you understand. You must be thinking I am crazy as I want you to invest in real estate with no money when real estate is so expensive, right? I thought the same but there is a way.

Steps to follow:

1) Know the market
2) Find the right real estate for you
3) Make a calculation
4) OPM (others people's money)
5) Make a deal

Know the Market

Before you start choosing the real estate you would like to buy, you should first decide in which area you want to focus. If you are planning to be renting real estate to students, professionals, businesses, etc... there will definitely be different strategies in all these areas. If you want, for example, to rent a flat to students, you want to make sure your flat is close to the university, close to the local bars as young people like to go and live in the city centre. Is there good night life? On the other hand, if you want to be renting to professionals you should be thinking, is the flat in a nice area? Is this area quiet at night? What about shops and transport? Do they have good access to local shops or to the train station so they can travel to work? Things like a sea or river view will add to the value. Does the flat have a garden? You need to decide which way your focus will go. Or if you want to rent real estate to businesses. Maybe you want to buy an empty shop and rent it out? This is also an option, but make sure the business who will be renting your shop has experience in that sector or you have a good contract. My focus is to buy a flat and rent it out to professionals. The reason why I have decided on this sector to start is that these people usually have a steady job (depends on your contract terms of course) which means they have a monthly income. Students are good too but usually they stay for shorter periods depending on how long they are studying, and they can be more messy than professionals. I am not saying everybody is the same, but have you ever visited a flat where students live? I did, that is why I have decided not to.

Find the right real estate

This step will probably be the longest one. There is so much real estate for sale. We need to find one where we will learn the fundamentals, and after we can repeat and repeat until we have as many as we want until we are finally financially free. Once we buy the first we will gain confidence. Where to look for real estate? There are many options where to look. Traditional ways are online. There are many real estate websites. Other places to look can be auction houses where real estate is usually cheaper. But remember, if you are in an auction the price can go higher so you need to do your calculations first before you decide to buy. Don't pay more than you have planned for.

Calculation

This part will take a little practise, but the more calculations you do the quicker you will become.

To understand calculations, we first need to know some basic real estate language.

FMV – Fair Market Value, it is the price for what you could possibly sell the real estate. Usually you can compare these prices with other similar sized properties in the same area.

LTV – Loan To Value, this is usually percentage. If you would want a mortgage the loan to value can be 90% of the cost of the property and the remaining 10% you would need to have as a deposit. But if you would like to buy and rent the property the loan to value is usually around 75%. It means you need to have a bigger deposit.

Monthly Repayments – the amount that you need to pay every month for your mortgage

APR – Annual Percentage Rate, it is the percentage the bank is charging every year for lending you money

Re-mortgage – it means you will take a new mortgage on your current mortgage. The reasons can be that you found a better mortgage with better APR, or your property increased in value and you are taking a new mortgage for the new value of the property

ROI – Return on investment

Calculation from the end

FMV = £50,000

LTV 75% = £37,500

Deposit 25% = £12,500

1) Annual amount of Mortgage (5%)   £1875
   Mortgage monthly   £156.25
   Management fees   £75
   Maintenance, Insurance   £75
   Total monthly outgoings   £306.25

2) Income
   Rent   £450/month

3) Monthly NET profit
   Total monthly income – total monthly outgoings = £143.75

Calculation number 2

LTV based on FMV – refurb costs - fees = maximum offer price
£37,500 - £4,000 - £2,000 = £30,500

Therefore LTV 75% = £22,875
Deposit 25%   = £7,625

Total Cash in:
25% deposit + refurb costs + fees = £13,625

After Re-mortgage and refinance
You will get back £14,625 – total cash in a deal
£13,625 = £1,000

£1,000 is your money what you earned as an extra that you made this deal possible

Now we can calculate our ROI

Yearly income (£143.75x 12)   £1,725

         ÷

Cash we put into a deal   £0

Our ROI   infinite

This is our calculation. I know it may sound difficult to start with, but the more calculations you make, the more you will understand. The main thing is to understand how this is working and how you can either re-mortgage your property and get money back from a deal or you could also sell the property and in this case it would look like this:

Your cash in a deal is the same £13,625

Your mortgage £22,875

You sell the property for £50,000

You pay back your mortgage and you pay back yourself the cash what you put into this deal and you will end up with £13,500. It is a good thing to get some capital for the start of your business, but remember that you need to reinvest this money if you don't want to pay taxes. If you keep this money it would be calculated as a capital gain and you will need to pay tax on it.

We want to acquire assets and build positive cashflow. In this case it is better to keep the property and have money come in every month from rent. I know £143.75/month is not much money, but if you did the same with ten properties you will have £1,437.5/month and this is good money in my opinion. You will do this until you achieve your own financial freedom.

OPM

Another thing is where to take this £13.625 for deposit, fees and refurb? Let's start with something you know and probably have. You may have your own credit card, right? Does your partner have one? Everybody has a different limit but I imagine you could have jointly around £5,000–£10,000 what you could use. There are companies which lend you money, some with good APR, some not so good, but if you make good calculations and timing you will be able to pay them back once the re-mortgage is done and this mean you won't pay all this interest as you will pay them back quicker. Just check which lenders are OK with paying back the money in a shorter period of time as some companies have hidden fees for full payment as they live on the fees. Or maybe you could ask your family or friends for the remaining money which you need in this deal. Always recalculate everything once you take a different loan as it can slightly change the outcome of your ROI. Have a look at this example:

Our cash in the deal £13,625

Credit cards	£5,000 (APR 30%)
Family, friends	£3,625 for easier counting (APR 0%)
Loan of remaining	£5,000 (APR 20%)

We will need this money for six months. We are able to refurb and re-mortgage this property. In six months we will get our money back.

Credit Cards £5,000 + 30% APR = £5,500 in one year, we return in six months £5,250

Monthly minimum payment 1% from the amount plus interest = £47

Loan £5,000 for five years monthly payment £132.47

We calculated that from beginning our monthly NET profit is £143.75/month. The first six months will be different as we didn't use our money.

Monthly NET income – credit card payment – loan payment = monthly profit/loss

£143.75 - £47 - £132.47 = -£35.72

In this situation we are losing £35.72 for the first six months. But after we re-mortgage, we pay back the loan, credit card and family. We are starting to generate our NET income of £143.75/month.

Our ROI in this situation will be slightly different.

Yearly income (£143.75 x 6 - £35.72 x 6)
£648.18

÷

Cash we put into a deal   £0

Our ROI   infinite

Make a deal

We did our research, we did our calculations, we think nothing can surprise us. An actual deal will make sure we are starting our financial freedom. It can be pretty straightforward but doesn't have to be. Especially if you decide to buy properties in an auction house. That is why we did our calculations. We know the FMV, we know how much we need to pay in fees and for refurb. We know the maximum we can offer. So if a property starts at £25,000 and you know you can't cross £30,500 to buy it, if someone offers more don't buy it. I know emotions are strong and you put a lot into it, did all the research, you calculated everything, but if you buy it for more you won't be able to have positive cashflow and have good

ROI. Write your number before you go to auction and don't go over it. It is good to have more flats you could potentially buy in one auction. If someone buys a property for more don't worry as you will have a chance to buy another one. And if all the properties are sold for more, don't worry. Start again, start your research, calculations, viewings, etc... The more you do, the more you will learn. I have never said that doing it this way will be quick or easy, but everybody can do it and we can eventually be financially free.

AREA 5

Growing

("Te only person you are destined to become is the person you decide to be." —Ralph Waldo Emerson)

This is a very important part of your life, because if you are not growing you are dying. This is something what we know as we were young. When we learned something new we were so excited and wanted more. Remember when you started to walk? How did you feel? I know you don't remember and I think most of us don't, but you know I have two daughters and the younger one started to walk and she is walking everywhere. She is so excited and she wants to go faster and she wants to be climbing everywhere, she is having the power and potential to learn everything and it is great. But while we are growing we are forgetting what the feeling is like as sometimes our parents, sometimes our teachers in school, are saying you can't do it or you can't do it in here. You are stupid, you are slow and much more. Somewhere on the way of growing we stop as we think we are not good enough and we do something which we feel confident we are able to do but this needs to stop. You need to find this secret power you have inside of you and this passion for growing, learning and accomplishing all the challenges you put for yourself. I recently changed my focus and found myself and I am constantly learning new things. I am growing and it gives me more and more power to the life I can share with others and it is a great feeling. I want you to do the same. Find something you love to do and go for it. Don't stop. Even if someone is telling you the opposite, don't listen to them. You have your own mind and you know you can achieve anything you desire. Growing is very important in our lives. Remember that.

AREA 6

Giving

*("Only those who have learned the power of sincere and selfless **contribution** experience life's deepest joy: true fulfilment." – Tony Robbins)*

This is a great part of our lives. As I stand for what Tony Robbins says: "Secret to living is giving". I can tell you a little bit of my story. When I started my business I was focused on myself and my family, and I was saying once I have more money I can give to someone, but not right now. But it takes a bit of time to get to this stage of your life that you have so much so you can give. I decided to give to a charity on a monthly basis even when I was struggling financially because I knew I would get there eventually, and there are people in bad situations over which they have no control. And once I started giving I felt better inside. I give even more now. I invited homeless people for Christmas dinner in my cafe and it was the best feeling I'd had in a long time as I could see the people in person and they could see that even strangers can care. Please don't forget to give to people on your way to the top. You can start by giving them your valuable time, you can volunteer if you don't have enough money just yet, but start now. And it will grow and grow and it will bring you happiness and you will be fulfilled in your life.

Once you balance all the areas in your life you will see the difference, how you feel and how happy you are and how happy the people around you are. Don't wait. Start right NOW.

This will be the end of my first book and I can't wait to write another one to share even more knowledge of what I will be learning from now on. Keep an eye on me and my projects so we can all go together to the next level. The only thing you need to do now is to start changing your mindset and grow. I know there are plenty of obstacles and disappointments on our way up but it is worth it.

My last bit of advice is: If you tell someone from your friends, family or colleagues what you are about to do with your life don't be disappointed as they may feel differently and they will try to bring you back down to earth, but think before you take their advice. The most important thing is from who is the advice coming from? Is it your single friend who is giving you advice on how to fix your relationship? Or a financial adviser who recommends you invest in a mutual fund who actually doesn't invest there himself? Think before you act. Thank you for your time reading this book. I am so happy.

BONUS

WANT TO KEEP WORKING TOGETHER BY JOINING MY TWO DAYS PROPERTY SECRETS MASTERMIND FOR JUST £75? (normal cost of this mastermind is £150)

YEAH, £75... CRAZY RIGHT? THIS IS A DEAL FOR YOU AS YOU TOOK THE TIME TO READ MY BOOK

I AM VERY HAPPY YOU DID, NOW IT IS TIME TO TAKE THE NEXT STEP TO YOUR FINANCIAL FREEDOM AND HAVE ALL THE TIME YOU WANT FOR YOUR FAMILY AND PARTNER

- I want to share my knowledge so we can go deep in this topic and you can learn faster to make money from properties.
- You don't need to spend lot of time learning and making mistakes in properties, but you can start properly and I will show you the way.
- I will show you how I started and my first deals.

And in case you are wondering, here is what a mastermind is:

It is collective genius of like-minded people sharing their knowledge while simultaneously learning from the leader of the group.

Learning from your own trial and error is painful, costly and simply outdated...

Masterminds are the answer and the new way to faster growth!!!

Just go to www.propertysecretsuk.com and watch the quick video sharing all the details about the mastermind, and I can't wait to work with you.

L - #0110 - 300120 - C0 - 210/148/3 - PB - DID2754343